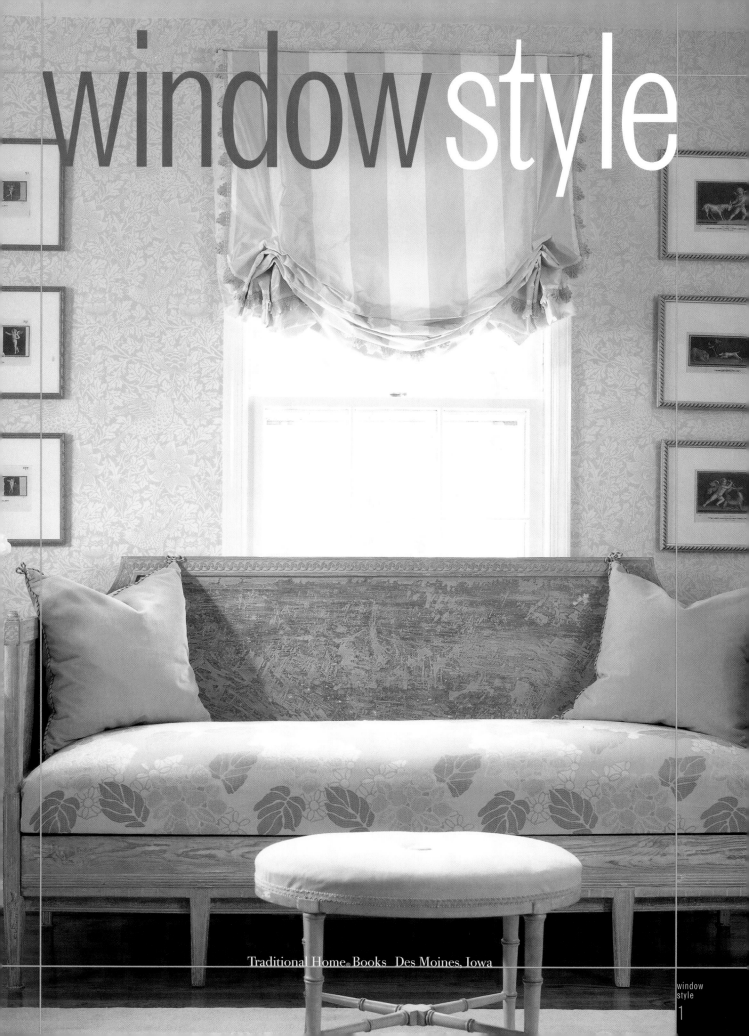

# window style

Traditional Home® Books  Des Moines, Iowa

Traditional Home® Books
An imprint of Meredith® Books

Traditional Home®
# window style

Editor: Linda Hallam
Senior Associate Design Director: Richard Michels
Contributing Editors: Heather Lobdell, Colleen Scully
Copy Chief: Terri Fredrickson
Copy and Production Editor: Victoria Forlini
Editorial Operations Manager: Karen Schirm
Managers, Book Production: Pam Kvitne, Marjorie J. Schenkelberg
Contributing Copy Editor: Jane Woychik
Contributing Proofreaders: Julie Cahalan, Becky Etchen, Erin McKay
Contributing Photographer: Gordon Beall
Indexer: Kathleen Poole
Electronic Production Coordinator: Paula Forest
Editorial and Design Assistants: Kaye Chabot, Karen McFadden, Mary Lee Gavin

## Meredith® Books
Publisher and Editor in Chief: James D. Blume
Design Director: Matt Strelecki
Managing Editor: Gregory H. Kayko
Executive Editor, Home Decorating and Design: Denise L. Caringer

Director, Operations: George A. Susral
Director, Production: Douglas M. Johnston

Vice President and General Manager: Douglas J. Guendel

## Meredith Publishing Group
President, Publishing Group: Stephen M. Lacy
Vice President-Publishing Director: Bob Mate

## Meredith Corporation
Chairman and Chief Executive Officer: William T. Kerr

Chairman of the Executive Committee: E. T. Meredith III

# {table of contents}

# introduction

# {create window style}

## About Window Treatments

My friends tease me about my passion for toile. It's true that I love the French scenic-print fabric so much that I have included at least one toile room in every decorating book I've written and every house I've owned. I liked the toile drapery panels in the bedroom of one house so much that I moved them with me halfway across the country to my current home, where they now frame glass doors in the dining room. Originally the tab-top panels gave my bedroom the privacy I needed—and enough darkness to sleep late on bright summer Saturdays. Now they are purely decorative, softening the sliding glass doors that lead to a porch.

At different times, these panels have served functional and decorative roles, the two reasons for using window treatments. People usually think of window treatments as a way to control light. As the Impressionist painters proved in the 19th century, light means everything. Their enduring paintings are among the most appealing art because the Impressionists knew how to capture light in oil and canvas. How a window treatment deals with the amount of natural light can truly mean the difference between a decorating scheme that works and one that fails.

## About *Window Style*

It's our goal in *Window Style* to give you a wealth of ideas—and popular and current styles—to help you make the best use of your windows and their fabric treatments. In creating *Window Style*, we worked with designers who meet these window challenges with taste and creativity. You'll find treatments that range from the classic styles of lavish swags and jabots to more tailored draperies and shades. You'll also find design solutions for every room in the house, as well as a whole-house scheme in designer Fiona Weeks' residence. To help you plan your own window treatments, we've included a chapter on working with design professionals.

As you look through *Window Style*, you'll see stunning examples of beautiful fabrics and trims and handsome hardware. You'll also see some smashing toiles. To me, it wouldn't be a decorating book—or a decorating scheme—without them.

Linda Hallam, Editor

dow style {all through the

house} window style wind

Whatever your personal style, the goal in decorating is quite simple: to create a home that is comfortable, beautiful, and personal, a refuge that feels good and lives well. Although the goal is simple, arriving at it is much more complicated. Knowing where to start, when to stop, and how to stay on track requires research, organization, and a long-range plan. Executing the plan requires smart decisions about furniture, fabric, and wall color, elements that create both continuity and individuality in a home.

So how do you begin choosing window treatments? A beautiful drapery design shown in a magazine or a book can inspire, but the design must be altered to suit your room's practical and aesthetic needs. Well-designed window treatments are specific to particular situations. This means that in addition to complementing the style of your home, its palette, and its furnishings, your designs should be tailored to the requirements of each window and what lies beyond it. For example, a treatment that exalts a glorious view is different from one that preserves sunlight while filtering harsh glare, and a design intended to visually lengthen a squatty window bears little resemblance to one that is destined to make the most of a room with high ceilings, moldings, and antique casements.

Interior designer Fiona Newell Weeks understands window treatments and the critical role they play in transforming mere rooms into unified, warm, and welcoming homes. She has moved three times during the past 10 years, decorating each of her houses from top to bottom along the way. Her latest home, a 1975 suburban clapboard not far from Washington, D.C., is shown in this chapter. Fiona and her husband fell in love with the tree-lined street, not the house itself. "We wanted a neighborhood full of children, a safe place where our boys could ride their bikes and play outdoors," she says. "There was nothing special about the house."

This house presented common design challenges: low ceilings, lack of architectural detail, and paltry natural light—all flaws that benefit from well-chosen window treatments. Fiona attacked the situation with crown molding, wide baseboards, wainscoting, and a "bright, fiery" palette featuring orange, yellow, and red mingled with accents of green, turquoise, and cream.

"Color is a great way to bring a sense of light to a dark house," Fiona says. "It is also conducive to good flow. I like to use the same colors throughout the first floor but change the dominance of the colors from room to room. It's easy on the eyes, yet it keeps things interesting."

In the living room, Fiona began with a boldly patterned rug that clearly defines the palette and sets a rich, invigorating mood. The furnishings and window treatments here harmonize rather than compete with the tone, pattern, and colors of the densely woven Oushak rug. "I am a firm believer

that one element—whether it's the rug, the walls, the furnishings, or the draperies—should draw your eye, while the others more quietly complement," Fiona explains. The carpet definitely is the focal point here, but the cantaloupe-hued flannel draperies at the windows are vividly beautiful and certainly eye-catching. The panels are interlined for opulence and mounted at the crown molding to encourage a sense of height.

In the adjoining dining room, the color scheme and focal point shift. Cantaloupe replaces red as the dominant hue, and the spotlight moves from the floor to the windows, where lemon yellow and cantaloupe cotton damask draperies with valances make an elegant, energetic statement. "Since dining rooms tend not to have as many furnishings or accessories, they are a terrific place to make a big statement with draperies," Fiona explains. The room's walls, also melon-hued, provide a dramatic backdrop for the drapery panels which are mounted at the crown molding. Together, the walls and draperies work to captivate the eye and distract from 8-foot ceilings.

The family room and breakfast area, which are on the same visual plane as the living room and dining room, perpetuate Fiona's warm color preferences. The family room is relaxed and casual, and the striped flat panels used at the bay window act as a striking frame for the room's focal point—a cozy window seat and a lovely view to mature trees beyond. Fiona strategically selected vertical stripes in muted reds, greens, orange, and cream to stretch the room skyward. For the breakfast area, between the dining room and family room, tailored, nonfunctional Roman shades adorn French doors. In rich sunflower yellow with embroidered birds, the shades lend restrained opulence to this clean-lined space and reinforce the first-floor palette.

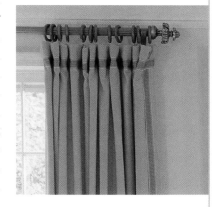

The bedrooms in this house are all upstairs. The palette relaxes here, and each room shares a common denominator—tranquility. "It's nearly impossible to achieve flow when you have a dainty girl's room next to a rough-and-tumble boy's room," Fiona says. However, she nonetheless managed to achieve continuity by using varied colors that are all of the same intensity. Furthermore, the two rooms visible from the top of the stairs (her daughter Tara's room and her son Griff's) are both blue, establishing a sense of order and calm at the entrance to the second floor.

Second-floor windows facing the street feature white wood blinds that provide privacy and a lovely consistency from the street. In the downstairs windows that face the street, Fiona created a different uniformity with long, straight drapery panels. "I think wooden blinds or shutters in every window, on both floors, could be overwhelming," she says. Each bedroom upstairs features weighty interlined draperies for warmth. "I want everyone to feel good in their own space, not just in the rooms we share downstairs," Fiona says. "Everyone, including young children, needs a comfortable personal refuge."

# supporting player

In a room where the Oushak rug sets the color palette and art makes a striking design statement, the cantaloupe-hued flannel draperies complement without competing with the scheme. In fact, by framing the abstract painting, the drapery panels call attention to a contemporary piece that balances the more traditional furnishings. Classic operable pinch-pleat draperies open and close easily courtesy of the rings and drapery rods. To visually raise the standard 8-foot ceiling, the lined and interlined panels are mounted at ceiling height and graze the floor.

Mounted inside the door trim, fixed Roman shades contribute embroidered pattern and cheerful yellow to a tailored breakfast room used for family dining. The fabric repeats on the seat cushions, an easy and classic way to unify a decorating plan. A more elaborate treatment fabricated from the same embroidered fabric might overwhelm a room, but here the careful use of the fabric as an accent enlivens the serene palette. Shades are mounted over a concealed cornice for a neat finish. Tasseled trim adds extra detailing and a sense of fun and whimsy to the neutral room.

softened with fabric

# star treatment

Because dining rooms often have minimal furnishings and accessories, window treatments lend themselves to notable roles. In a dining room graced by a double-pedestal table and traditional dining chairs, lushly gathered lemon yellow and cantaloupe cotton damask draperies, lined and interlined for shape and proper hanging, pair with neatly pleated, matching valances. Flat trim adds detailing that defines the tailored fabrication. The treatment is mounted at ceiling height to showcase the rich fabric and to add importance to a room with a standard 8-foot ceiling.

}

# elegantly casual chic

Where softness and finish are desired but complete coverage isn't a must, a fixed balloon shade can introduce just the right touch of a favored fabric to the scene. (A fixed balloon can also conceal a shade or blinds that can be lowered when light control or privacy is needed.) In this sitting area, the trimmed balloon supports but doesn't overshadow the stunning leaf print that covers the bench cushion. The striped fabric belongs to the happy yellow color family that dominates the space; the wallpaper introduces another secondary pattern. Solid-yellow pillows balance the array of stylish patterns.

Flat, striped drapery panels, sewn to rings for operability, frame the bay window in the family room. The panels are floor-length, a graceful statement that avoids the sometimes choppy, bisected appearance of panels that reach only to the window seat. Here the panels hang easily from an exposed rod supported by a center bracket. Turned horizontally, the stripe serves as matching trim for the panels, giving them a polished look. The stripe reappears as upholstery for the English-style ottoman, a comfortable piece that adds to the coziness of this pillow-filled room.

}

framing the view

A pretty, nicely detailed window treatment adds a special welcome to a guest room. For a bedroom with an old-fashioned feel, a scalloped valance overlies drapery panels sewn from a novelty print with green background. The valance and drapery panels attach by rings to an iron rod featuring decorative finials. Greek-key trim stitched to the edges of the panels is an appropriate finishing touch that echoes the classical motifs of the fabric. Tasseled rope tiebacks gently hold the panels in place, creating a soft fullness that works with the romantic feel of the inviting room. Framed art, flanking the window, completes the setting.

charm welcomes guests

# tailored for the master

For a master bedroom furnished with quiet, tasteful appointments, drapery panels introduce subtle pattern and color without overwhelming fabrication. Lined and interlined for warmth and graceful hang, the panels graze the neutral carpet; they are sewn to rings for a traditional operable treatment. The fabric contributes interest to the room and is tailored enough to comfortably share the space with solid, tufted chairs and a traditional chest. White wood blinds, pulled up during the day, ensure privacy without adding the distraction of another fabric treatment.

}

# classic for a boy's room

{ Fun rooms call for lighthearted walls—and window treatment fabrics. In a home of classic good taste, this boy's room features a playful interpretation of traditional blue: horizontal-striped painted wall finish and drapery panels fabricated from an inventive leaf-print fabric. The panels hang by fabric ties from the exposed rod—a treatment that won't be outgrown too quickly. The folded-fabric border in snappy, complementary stripes finishes the drapery panels in tailored style, elevating a standard treatment into a classic accompaniment suitable for any age.

toile accompaniments

In a bedroom where ever-popular toile sets the romantic scene, creamy white drapery panels edged in a flat braid enhance the color palette while providing visual relief from the stylized pattern. The goblet-header drapery panels, sewn to white rings, slide easily on the painted white drapery rod. The exposed rod is visually more open and often is a fresher look than a fabric-covered rod or cornice. Simple touches, such as the flat braid, give a neatly finished look to drapery panels. Wood blinds are virtually invisible when pulled up, but provide privacy and light control as needed.

window style {draperies and

curtains}window style wir

There are no window treatments more classic than draperies. Draperies bring a wonderful sense of luxury, warmth, and beauty to a room—and when done well, they exceed these high expectations. In the best cases, draperies complete a room, making an otherwise appealing room even more irresistible. In the worst cases, draperies miss the point, seem awkward, or are poorly crafted. Carefully planning a drapery treatment will ensure that it suits your room and lives up to your dreams.

What is the difference between a drapery and a curtain? Sometimes the two terms are used interchangeably, but the difference is very simple: Curtains are short treatments; draperies are full-length. With some exceptions, a curtain will be a simpler, more casual treatment.

Draperies are especially good at softening large windows that would seem cold, hard, or harsh if left unadorned. Draperies provide excellent insulation, privacy, and light control. Draperies elegantly frame beautiful views or distract the eye from views you'd rather not see. And when creatively conceived, draperies have the power to transform even the ugliest duckling windows into truly graceful swans. Whether your windows are short and squat, too narrow, or too plain, a savvy drapery will give them—and your entire room—a totally new attitude.

The best draperies are those that are most compatible with an individual room. Part of creating compatibility is realizing that windows come with distinct shapes, styles, and needs. Rather than preselecting a drapery treatment (and fabric and hardware) and forcing it upon a window, work with or for a particular window to create a treatment that amplifies the window's assets and downplays its flaws.

The other half of compatibility involves making draperies that work for the room as a whole. This requires consideration of several factors: the architecture of the room, the furnishings, the palette, the mood of the room, and how the room will be used. Making draperies work for a room can mean making a splashy contrasting statement at the windows or designing treatments that blend with the interiors. Practical rules apply: Steer clear of draperies in kitchens and bathrooms, where dampness, grime, and high traffic can cause premature aging of fabrics. Common sense also applies: Choose designs and fabrics that are appropriate for your rooms. Opulent damask panels would look strange in a room showcasing 1950s modern furnishings. And gauzy draperies hung from chrome clips along a stainless-steel cable would seem bizarre in a Colonial home of 18th-century antiques. There is plenty of room to play, to stray, to "push the envelope," and it is this kind of bravura that often leads to something very special—and very satisfying. Yet there are basic parameters, and unless you have a great deal of design experience, it is always best to adhere to these.

There are draperies to suit every decorative style. Draperies designed for formal rooms are most often made with fabrics that convey luxury. Silk, damask, and chintz are perennial favorites that will enhance any formal room. Dressmaker details—including undulating goblet pleats, spiffy contrast cuffs, tiny knife pleats, exuberant ruffles, and passementerie (thick tassels, rich trims and cording, wood or crystal beading, and other jewelrylike accents)—amplify the effect of a dressy fabric and lend a true couture feeling to a window treatment and room. A fancy valance will heighten the impression of any formal drapery treatment. These techniques and trimmings are costly, but when executed beautifully they make a room feel sublime. They are investments in window treatments that you will love to live with for years to come.

A formal look doesn't have to be expensive, however. Experienced designers know that well-chosen drapery hardware can convey a formal look for less money. When budgets are a consideration, designers use simple drapery panels constructed of attractive, affordable fabrics (cottons and linens work well) and pair them with statement-making hardware such as burnished golden rods, silvered pineapple finials, or antique tiebacks. Imagine persimmon-hued cotton panels mounted with rings on a slender wrought-iron rod and rings tipped with antique arrow finials; or picture quilted linen panels paired with an ebony-stained pole and golden rings. These two examples, plucked from show houses, look stunning in a formal setting, without a stunning price tag.

Draperies for casual rooms are generally simpler and more relaxed. They use less opulent fabrics and details. This doesn't mean draperies slated for casual rooms should be plain—the best ones aren't. Even relaxed ones benefit from a little "Aha!" Whether it's an appealing contrast lining, a jaunty trim or tape, or an unusual rod, some feature should give each treatment panache. Try an old rowboat oar, a pitchfork, or giant bamboo as a drapery rod; adorn a natural linen panel with tiny seashells along the leading edges; or mount architectural salvage as unexpected drapery brackets, finials, or dramatic cornices.

As for curtains, these abbreviated draperies are most often associated with kitchens, breakfast areas, bathrooms, little girls' rooms, and other casual settings. We all know about cafe curtains; they're intimately associated with country-style decorating. But there are all sorts of appealing departures from this basic theme. Depending on the fabrics used, the hardware selected, and the tailoring and trim, curtains take on all sorts of moods, from traditional to modern and from funky to ultrachic. Whatever style you choose, never skimp on fabric—fullness and repeat guarantee curtain success.

# scalloped and trimmed

{ In a room where tradition and refined taste reign, the scalloped motifs of the drapery panels and the upholstered armchair echo the curved shapes of the Chippendale-inspired coffee table and antique chair. The scalloped, trimmed detailing visually divides the drapery panels into thirds, a pleasing and classic design proportion. The soft yellow silk fabric, lined for shape, adds another grace note. Panels are gathered on painted rods hung directly below crown molding. Such installation adds importance to a treatment and visually extends window height to beautiful proportions.

A classic, document-style print balances the richly detailed moldings and candle chandelier in a beautifully appointed living room of a period home. Because the upholstered fabrics are solids and tone-on-tone silk, the lush drapery fabric imbues the room with stylish warmth appropriate to the setting. The tailored pinch-pleat style, without ornate hardware or top treatments, allows the detailed, realistic patterns and motifs to be viewed clearly and enjoyed. Installation, below the gold-leaf egg-and-dart molding, contributes to the grand effect. Accent pillows trimmed in braid repeat the drapery fabric for a unified design.

# repeating a lavish print

{ The finishing touch of gracefully swagged, tasseled cording elevates a handsome window treatment into a refined design statement that complements a richly furnished living room and calls attention to a pair of small paintings. The cording repeats the sunny yellow and cool blue of the silk drapery fabric; the subtle wall stripe and the tinted ceiling echo the color scheme. Drapery panels, sewn with rod pockets for a tailored presentation, are gathered on a fluted rod installed below the dentil molding. Decorative finials, also fluted and detailed, finish in high style reminiscent of the neoclassic period.

# braided and tasseled

# gold clips for pinch pleats

In a tailored, library-style sitting room, neutral drapery panels soften the tall windows, contribute texture, and close for nighttime warmth—without the distraction of pattern or contrasting color. The panels, which slightly puddle, provide coverage without undue fullness. For subtle sophistication and practical opening and closing, the lined panels are sewn to tiny gold-tone clips which contrast with the black iron rod. These small touches of gold and black reinforce other accents in the room, such as the coffee table, oval frame, and black and gold accessories.

}

# dressed up with jabots

Though often chosen for their tailored good looks, drapery panels can take on the flourishes of more detailed treatments with the judicious inclusion of such details as swags and jabots. In a room with pairs of French doors, dressy fixed panels in a bold yet traditional print define door frames and add enriching color and pattern. Panels are attached behind crown molding that was installed as part of the window treatment. The swag and jabot detailing gives a pretty, dressmaker finish to a room where curvy armchairs sport ruffled skirts and the sofa dons deep fringe.

{ Taupe drapery panels and hardware introduce pleasing pattern and an additional hint of color that warms a traditional room of cool neutrals. The emphasis is on the fabric, which is lined for shape and fullness; fabrication is simple and reserved—tailored pinch pleats sewn to standard rings. The dark rod and rings reinforce other dark accents in the room, such as the tables, the exposed woodwork on the furniture, and the contemporary-style table lamp. The same fabric, in a blue colorway, appears as accent pillows for the window seat. Off-white Roman shades add extra privacy and temperature control.

# pair a print with shades

# pale panels balance art

Where contrast between classic and contemporary style is the goal, simple linen panels edged with mahogany bell trim flank the dramatic modernistic painting. Although the windows are tall in the grand space, the designer chose to hang the panels directly below the crown molding to emphasize the vertical form of the art. Noteworthy for their tailored quality, the draperies add a sense of restrained formality because they hang neatly, on gold-tone clips, from a white rod. Working together, the creamy white draperies and furniture create graphic tension against the espresso brown walls and colorful art.

# floor-length window style

Opaque fabric stretched neatly between swing-arm drapery rods forms stylized drapery panels that combine the ideas of indoor shutters and casement windows. The design ensures coverage and sun control for floor-to-ceiling windows without obscuring the fluted trim. In a setting where moldings and raised paneling abound, the understated treatment avoids jarring contrast of color or pattern and lets architectural details and dramatic furnishings take the lead role. At the same time, the effect is light and airy, a fresh take for a decidedly formal setting.

# cornice crowns silk panels

In a room inspired by the Art Deco style of 1930s ocean liners, lushly full pinch-pleated satin draperies hang behind cornice boards, blending two different styles of window configurations for a unified backdrop and subtle sophistication. In keeping with graphic Deco style, free-form silk bands in an oversize trellis pattern embellish the lined panels. The pale, creamy satin creates a wall of fabric that showcases appropriate furnishings, including tuxedo sofas, a 4-foot-tall urn with hidden spotlight, and zigzag tables. The panels also give the room a romantic sense of enclosure.

# cafe style, sunny scene

{ Lighthearted cafe curtains solve the dilemma of how to treat arch-topped, Palladian-style windows in a casual setting where sun control isn't paramount. The curtains, in a sheer windowpane fabric, provide the needed privacy without blocking light or covering up the handsome windows. For minimum fuss and maximum style, curtains attach with red drapery rings to turned, decorative rods dressed with finials. The touch of red repeats the room's accent color; the subtle green of the windowpane is a secondary accent color in the lively scheme.

{ Draperies can define rooms or alcoves when the panels are used as portieres, the French term for curtains hung across doorways. For this secluded nook at the end of a hall, the portiere panels create a sense of enclosure to make an open space comfortable for a private chat. The banded silk panels are hung from rods at ceiling height and held in place with tiebacks. Opaque panels at the window give privacy and a further sense of enclosure without adding the competition of color or pattern. The two styles of panels contrast but visually blend for a pleasing design.

portiere defines setting

# fitting the curve with style

For a dining room design inspired by the great English country houses, a pair of goblet-headed pleated drapery panels crisscross to fit the exacting dimensions of a dramatic Palladian-style window. Panels are edged in a jabot-type banded trim in keeping with the dressmaker touches of English style; the panels are held in place with tasseled, corded silk tiebacks. The installation inside the window arch ensures that the full beauty of the detailing, including the classic Greek key motifs, will be savored. The treatment softens a room of rich paneling and frames the view while introducing tailored detailing.

# up-to-the-ceiling chic

Designed to be quiet and restful, this serene guest room takes its cue from walls upholstered in an ecru-beige silk-linen blend. The carpeting, furniture, and window treatment were chosen for minimum contrast, and the room relies on a variety of textures versus colors to intrigue the eye. Although quiet is key, the room reinforces sophisticated sensibilities with the choices of neutral shades, fabric, and fabrication. Tightly gathered with a header on a painted rod that is hung at ceiling height, the ballgown-style drapery panels of silk taffeta can be closed, but more utilitarian blinds provide privacy and light control.

{ An antique, Napoleon-style bed with canopy sets the scene, and pink and black set the color scheme in a youthful bedroom. Dressed in a Swedish linen fabric with freehand flowers, the bed is the obvious star. Pink and white checked taffeta panels reinforce the color choice while providing needed privacy and sun control. Because of its body, taffeta holds its shape well for the simple yet stylish panels, which skim the floor without puddling. To allow easy opening and closing, the panels are sewn to brass rings on matching drapery rods. A center bracket supports the rod over the wide windows.

# fresh colors for fun

# tab ties go sophisticated

The simplicity of unlined, tie-on tab panels relaxes a bedroom where rich red and traditional furniture contrast with crisp white. Instead of the typical two-panels-per-window application, one tab panel per window imbues the setting with a casual, romantic insouciance—an appropriate mood in a room where the fine furnishings, including an antique bed and French-style chairs, aren't taken too seriously. To keep the look on the casual side, the designer chose to install the forged-iron rods between the window casings and the crown molding, allowing ample contrast between the white elements and the deep red walls.

# happy colors and curves

In a child's room, bright and bold horizontal stripes and a wonderfully curvy canopy set the scene. The window treatment echoes the look with tightly woven cotton drapery panels of equally colorful, though condensed, stripes in hot pink and orange and a curved iron rod. Sewn to small iron rings, the panels drape to create their own unstructured heading, a casual look appropriate to the youthful setting. Although rarely closed, the panels are full and long enough to pull over the window if desired. The playful stripe repeats as tailored Roman shades for French doors that lead to the garden.

# banded and trimmed

{ Planned strictly for design interest in a quietly neutral master bedroom, these fixed, banded drapery panels eschew the standard ring-and-rod installation in favor of an innovative combination of grommets and wall-mount hooks. The treatment adds dimension and soft draping to the silk panels, and the flat braid above and below the wide gray band contributes a polished finish. The lined panels slightly puddle for elegant softness. Because the panels are fixed, natural woven shades do the practical work, controlling privacy and light without introducing color or obvious pattern to the room.

In a contemporary twist on classic American patchwork, wool fabric softens the modern style of a city bedroom. The operable panels, banded in off-white and sewn to chrome rings, slide easily on the unadorned chrome rod. The subtle differences between shades of gray and taupe wool play off the rich brown walls, the neatly tied linen headboard, and the white bed linens; the chrome rod echoes the finish on the stylized floor lamp. Three narrow blinds meet the need for privacy while the unlined textured wool fabric filters light and views with easy, unstructured style.

# color-block contemporary

# knotted and tied for style

In a ladylike bedroom inspired by 18th-century American colonial houses, fabric and fabrication create an appropriately dressy window treatment. Because privacy was not a concern in the country-house setting, the interior designer chose to repeat the bed skirt's tone-on-tone Italian silk blend for the drapery panels. The cutouts in the fine fabric add decorative touches to the formal treatment. In keeping with the graceful look, the unlined panels are simply gathered and tied over the rod and allowed to slightly puddle on the floor. Pineapples—a popular 18th-century symbol of hospitality—appear as finials on each rod.

window style

cornices}window style wi

In many cases, valances and cornices are like icing on a cake. When done well, these classic top treatments, so often paired with formal drapery panels, make something beautiful all the more so. Not long ago, it seemed that almost every formal window treatment was crowned by a complex valance adorned with tassels, trim, ruffles, and rosettes. All this has changed. Decorating in general, including even very formal traditional design, is cleaner and crisper now, and opulence for opulence's sake has been replaced by a simpler, pared-down sense of luxury. Even in the most dressed-up interior settings today, graceful drapery panels can stand on their own.

This being said, it is also true that the valance and its wood or metal counterpart, the cornice, are both alive and well and looking better than ever, especially in rooms that favor traditional style. Valances and cornices may not be as heavily laden with passementerie as during years past, but the well-edited finery is chic, the dressmaker details are exquisite, and the combinations of fabrics are fresh and sophisticated. Valances and cornices remain one of the most glorious ways to express a sense of luxury, formality, and unabashed beauty in any traditional room.

Valances and cornices are naturally versatile. We tend to think of them first as elegant partners to classic draperies, but they work in many other situations. For instance, valances and cornices combine harmoniously with blinds, including wood and matchstick blinds. A valance-and-blind combination is suitable for many rooms in the house, but it's an especially smart pairing in kitchens, baths, and mudrooms, high-traffic zones where dampness and dirt make full-length draperies impractical. In these settings, the softness of a valance or an upholstered cornice often provides much-needed counterpoint to the preponderance of hard surfaces.

If your budget is a factor, a valance or cornice can give you a luxurious look that is far less pricey than draperies are. A favorite fabric can be fashioned into a valance or cornice and paired with a blind or a roller shade for an affordable combination of beauty and practicality. The fabric can even be an expensive one, because you won't need yards and yards. The blind or shade may not be the apex of aesthetics, but it will do the job—providing excellent light control and privacy when called upon and remaining discreetly hidden beneath the valance or cornice until needed. In fact, valances or cornices are often used in bedrooms to conceal blackout shades.

Valances and cornices also can go it alone to make a grand design statement. Like drapery panels, a stand-alone valance or cornice can be a lovely choice for windows that are well-proportioned, attractive, and located where there are no light control or privacy concerns. In this situation, and when you have windows leading the eye to spectacular views, a valance or cornice can lend the right measure of decoration—a stylish touch that can soften and frame the window without distracting from the beauty of the window itself or competing with the natural beauty of the view just beyond it.

Designing a valance or cornice requires care and expertise. The top treatment needs to relate to the proportions of the window, of course, but it must also work with the ceiling height, the room dimensions, and any additional window treatment that may accompany it. The design of all but the simplest of valances is best left to a professional—an expert who knows whether it will be best to hang the valance at the crown molding or right above the window, someone who will be able to advise you regarding the virtues of inverted pleats and other dressmaker details and introduce you to fabrics and embellishments that will complement your room and enhance its overall style and mood.

An experienced decorator may also advise you regarding the hows and whys of introducing an unusual cornice. Most cornices are constructed of plywood that is papered, painted, or padded and upholstered. Other cornices can be made from one-of-a-kind architectural salvage or from tin and other metals. Some cornices are artfully faux-painted, and some have fanciful shapes. In nurseries, children's rooms, and playrooms, a cornice can be a great tool for injecting a good dose of fun.

Designers love valances and cornices. They admit that these treatments can be costly and that valances and cornices aren't appropriate for every situation. These are decorative treatments that showcase a design professional's creativity—his or her ability to unite facing and lining fabrics, pleating styles, and passementerie to create something beautiful and original for your room. Of course, if your valance or cornice is utterly simple, you may choose to create your own. However, because of the need to ensure that valances and cornices are properly scaled to the window, the ceiling height, and the room's dimensions, it's usually best to leave their design and fabrication to professional interior designers and workrooms.

MARTIN HARRISON

# points for whimsy

Even in a staunchly traditional room, a little whimsy goes a long way. Side-by-side valances with staggered jester points in tangerine and cream silk smooth the rough edges created by two unlike windows placed uncomfortably close together. The valance motif provides light counterpoint to some serious antique furniture. The valance hues, plucked from the room's understated dotted wallpaper, play richly to the luminous wood tones. The valance points are adorned with pearly tangerine beads that echo the dots of the wallpaper. The smaller valance is paired with a sheer panel depicting colonial figures.

}

These handsome hand-painted cornices help give a plain, dark, and low-ceiling living room a new attitude. Floors and ceilings, both painted in cream, lighten and brighten. Tone-on-tone green striped walls pair with a wallpaper border that mimics elaborate crown molding; together they visually elevate the ceiling and create a smart foundation for a room that is now anything but plain. The classically styled cornices harmonize with the room's palette and add a crisp architectural touch. The old-gold scroll motif plays up the room's architectural mood and interjects a hint of opulence.

# interjecting opulence

# lamp shade luxe

Conjuring images of pagodas and old-fashioned silk lampshades, these richly detailed valances delight the eye and reiterate the undulating curves of the sofa and side table. The fanciful valances provide lovely balance to the hard lines of the handsome dentil molding and wainscoting. In a room that is full of inviting color and texture but mostly devoid of pattern, the valances' complex toile fabric introduces important and ample interest. The deep bullion fringe overlaid with beaded accents plays up the pagoda shape of the valances and adds soft richness to the room.

# hand-painted beauty

In this intimate sitting room, the cornice takes center stage and shines. Featuring Chinese Chippendale motifs, the hand-painted cornice plays up the room's garden-fresh hues, including mossy green walls, a rose red love seat, and a daffodil yellow ceiling. The large-scale patterns of the cornice contrast elegantly with the diminutive red check adorning the drapery panels. Mounting the cornice at the crown molding creates the impression of floor-to-ceiling windows. Extending the cornice across the width of the small room and pairing it with drapery panels unifies and broadens the pair of slender windows.

Silk tassels trimmed in gold and brown hues define this classic and refined window treatment featuring an upholstered cornice mounted high at the ceiling. The creamy white cornice and drapery panels might at first glance seem designed to blend subtly with the golden maize walls. Yet they create precisely the opposite effect, shining brightly and becoming, in contrast with the saturated wall color, a dramatic and unexpected focal point. The silk tassel trim emphasizes the graceful arch of the cornice, a shape that is useful for boosting architectural interest in a traditional-style room.

# neo classic geometry

{ Vibrant valances amplify the neoclassic mood of this sitting room. Deep window reveals are framed by full-panel folding shutters painted the same gray-green as the room's elegant woodwork, walls, and ceiling. The gray-green hue provides a serene backdrop against which valances become gracious scene-stealers. Fitted neatly inside the deep window wells, the valances feature striking cutout borders that captivate the eye and repeat the geometry of the painted floor. Opaque shades pull down from behind the valances to cut glare and effectively put too-close neighbors out of sight and mind.

# fabrication as art

These artfully constructed valances enhance the beauty of an exuberantly pattern-filled study. The dark ground of the valances and their matching panels complements the fireplace tiles and helps anchor this high-ceilinged space. The print plays to hues throughout the room. The arched valances, which are hung high at the deep crown molding, feature elegant inverted pleats and illustrate the importance of skillful fabrication: Despite the pleats, the pattern of the complex botanical print is uninterrupted. A dark fabric is sewn within the pleats; the intentionally visible contrast lining is bright cranberry.

In a sun-drenched room with stunning windows, the touch of softness provided by this wraparound valance ensures the perfect finish. Although the expanse of windows might seem cold and harsh if left bare, a heavy drapery would be cruel and unusual treatment. The valance's lyrical garland motif contrasts aesthetically with the mullioned panes; the brilliant colors of the fabric form a lovely frame for a lush garden view. The valance is paired with strictly ornamental panels in the same rich fabric. Imparting added grace and easy yet sophisticated style, the panels are positioned in the corners to preserve sunlight.

}

# wrapped with a valance

# exotic easygoing chic

Vivid color and geometric pattern generate drama in a formerly plain-Jane room. Maize-colored walls, a lichen-hued ceiling, and silvery stencils work together to create architectural interest. The persimmon and melon silk handkerchief valances enhance the lively, friendly feeling. Paired with loosely woven blinds that admit sunlight while providing privacy, these fresh and shimmery valances drape over metal rods mounted above the window tops, giving the impression of taller windows. The valances are trimmed with geometric charms that echo motifs found throughout the playful room.

# tailored take on toile

In this attic guest room with small dormer windows, preserving natural light and multiplying its effect was key. Simple valances featuring bright yellow cotton toile lined with taupe linen provide a tailored softness that looks stunning but doesn't hinder sunshine. The handkerchief-style valances, which are simply draped over cherry rods, coordinate happily with the invigorating striped wallpaper that climbs the angular walls. The toile at the window is repeated on an accent pillow and the bed's duvet. A sconce, a pair of armless chairs, and a marble-top table complete the chic scene.

This playful, colors-of-the-rainbow valance stretches across four tall windows and vividly illustrates how important an inspired window treatment can be in creating a room that looks good and lives well. Minus the spirited pennant-style valance, with its dangling beaded points, this could be a ho-hum room, one that would barely merit notice. The sofa's accent pillows enhance the lively and colorful effect. A valance like this can work beautifully with no other treatment when a room has no need for privacy or light control. In this case, simple white sheers can close to fend off glare without stealing attention from the valance.

spirited pennants

# light look for traditional

Dining rooms often are spaces where window treatments take a turn to the very elaborate and highly ornate. In comparison, these gracefully pleated valances with cascading jabots are fairly simple and straightforward, harmonizing with a room punctuated by garden-fresh colors and motifs. These light-preserving valances, fashioned from silk striped in green, red, and yellow, feature bright contrast lining and gathered headers piped in the same bright fabric. The bottom hems are treated with rich fringe that complements the valance hues and the other pretty fabrics in the room.

# pugs and pattern

{ In a kitchen designed for a couple with eight canine housemates, crisp color blocks created by bright white cabinetry and rich red walls are further energized by imaginative valances that celebrate dogs and serve up delicious pattern and playfulness. Mounted inside the window frames in order to showcase elegant moldings, the valances feature pugs striking various poses, framed by a relaxed plaid that cascades softly to reveal sparkling red contrast lining. Above the kitchen sink, two valances adjoin to create a darling double treatment that unifies the two attractive windows.

chapter

window style {swags and

jabots} window style wind

You may be wondering how a swag differs from a valance or cornice—a fine question indeed. The three top treatments are closely related. Each stands alone nicely, but more often, these treatments are paired with draperies, shades, shutters, or blinds. The terms swag and valance are sometimes used interchangeably, but a swag can be distinguished by its close, open relationship to its hardware. While valances and cornices hide their own workings as well as those of any accompanying treatments, a swag may incorporate the drapery rod, finials, brackets, and other hardware that it utilizes as an integral part of the design statement. Top treatments such as swags offer a practical application as well: For bedrooms or other rooms where privacy or blackout shades are needed, the fabric at the top conceals the utilitarian shade when the shade isn't in use. In such cases, the swag needs to be lined to ensure maximum coverage.

Swags work best when windows are attractive and proportional. Unlike a valance or cornice, which can hide (and correct) a multitude of sins, a swag leaves little room for illusion, openly celebrating the window as is. Swag styles, like those of valances and cornices, run the gamut from formal and historical to casual and contemporary. Formal swags—classic treatments well-suited to traditional homes with high ceilings and good architecture—may combine opulent facing and lining fabrics, lush passementerie, and dressmaker details that all work to draw the eye toward a window and the view beyond. Silk facing fabrics are often lined with complementary colored and patterned fabrics that stand up better to intense sunshine. Antique textiles, such as vintage toiles, antique damasks, and heirloom embroideries, create lyrical and individual formal statements. These types of swags usually look best when interlined. A plain or patterned sheer adorned with crystal beading has a filmier effect, filtering sunlight throughout the day and introducing ephemeral beauty.

Swags may be shaped simply, like scarves, or have sophisticated designs featuring soft folds or tighter ruching, cascading tails, or jabots. Pleating, too, is often part of the handsome fabrication. For all but the simplest designs, consulting a design professional makes good sense. But determining the shape, size, fabrics, and trimmings of a swag is only half of the equation; making smart hardware choices is also key. In rooms where the style is

decidedly dressy, a gold-leaf, silvered, ebony-stained, or painted rod can be used to make a rich, substantial statement. For more relaxed formality with a bit of contrast, a hand-forged iron rod can make a fresh and attractive choice. The addition of shapely finials also may heighten the effect. In casual settings, simple wood rods or unusual materials—architectural salvage, bamboo, an aspen tree branch, or even an old rowboat oar—can serve as artful partners to drapery swags.

Mounting a swag can be as simple as draping it over or wrapping it along a decorative rod. Brackets, finials, tiebacks, or rosettes mounted high on each side of the window or attractively spaced across the top of a window frame are other options for mounting formal or casual swags. Ready-made products are available for these types of mountings, but the most effective mountings are often customized to suit the design of the window treatment and the room. In casual settings, such as children's rooms or nurseries, drawer pulls, antique doorknobs, unusual hooks or rings, vintage tableware, and other imaginative items can be adapted.

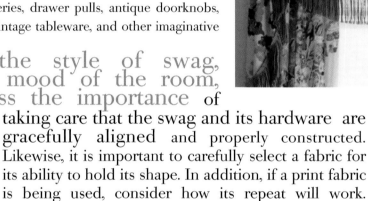

Whatever the style of swag, whatever the mood of the room, designers stress the importance of taking care that the swag and its hardware are gracefully aligned and properly constructed. Likewise, it is important to carefully select a fabric for its ability to hold its shape. In addition, if a print fabric is being used, consider how its repeat will work. Smaller florals or other patterns in a modest scale work well for loosely draped swags. Classic fabrics, such as cotton or linen toiles, also are often used for this graceful treatment. If two different fabrics are used in a combination treatment (swag with drapery or drapery with valance), their weights and their degrees of formality should be compatible for a pleasing look and presentation. In such an application, the swag may be the more detailed fabric, such as silk taffeta plaid, and the drapery panels may be fabricated in a solid color pulled from the swag.

In rooms with French doors or with an assortment of window styles, such as double-hung casements, swags with or without draperies may be used on one style of window or door. A tailored Roman shade or other variation may work best on another style of window in the same room. To enhance the beauty of a swag treatment in such settings, bullion fringe or other trim is often incorporated in the swag and repeated on the other window treatments.

# making a statement

{ In an elegant room of grand proportions, a glamorous yet understated treatment—lined silk taffeta in layers of peachy champagne and celadon green—frames tall windows and reflects the soft champagne color of the painted walls. Belgian linen shades, trimmed in green silk and mounted inside the decorative treatment, can be pulled down for sun control. Decorative tiebacks hold the top swags in place and echo the carved moldings and ornate mirror frames. For a luxurious finish, the side panels lavishly puddle, as do the silk table skirts.

# traditional style refined

A beautifully fabricated swag-and-jabot treatment complements and finishes a room where classic traditional is the desired look. Inspired by rooms of the 18th century, this sitting room uses a painted floor as a stylish stand-in for a carpet and a mural as a scenic focal point. The color of the swag's toile-type print of taupe and daffodil yellow reinforces the sunny qualities of the room and introduces the primary pattern. Jabots are lined with a taupe checked fabric, which relaxes the style. In keeping with the nod to tradition, the inner jabot grazes the top of the lower sash while the outer jabot brushes the top of the window seat.

# swagged from rosettes

{ When the design goal is a pretty, traditional room, a window treatment fabricated with dressmaker detailing provides the right touch. In a living room with a playful bent, swags are gathered in the full, lush style of Austrian shades and attached with rosettes. Behind, the cornice board is neatly finished in a large-scale plaid. Fringed trim adds another layer of detailing. Jabots, lined in plaid, neatly frame the bay window and call attention to the inviting window seat. The repetition of the plaid fabric unifies the room, with visual relief provided by large doses of white and the open-ground trellis-pattern carpet.

As an alternative to an exposed drapery rod, scalloped swags attach over a concealed cornice board for a finished look that features the pleasing details of bullion trim and fanciful fabric rosettes. Because of the width of the window, a series of swags is more visually pleasing than one or even two swags. Side panels, without jabots, frame the wide, fixed window and call attention to the painting behind the camelback sofa. The floral fabric softens the scene, contrasting with the more tailored upholstery fabrics while reinforcing the room's lively palette.

}

# graceful swag as cornice

# tied tassels and tails

{ Swags and jabots disguise odd window placement and wide, chunky molding—and lighten a living room of dark oak paneling. The swag treatment allows light to stream in, and the contrast between the classic toile and the jaunty miniprint distracts the eye from the awkward placement of the windows. The toile fabric matches the brown-on-ivory wallpaper, chosen to brighten but still complement the dark oak. The jabots effectively cloak the wide window trim. Chenille tassels tied with cording stylishly accent the cotton fabrics.

# fancy for deep fringe

To warm a room of large proportions, lushly draped swags and jabots are fabricated from a classic floral silk and trimmed with deep fringe. The dressy treatment is an appropriate fashion-forward statement in a room with a mix of antiques, such as the neoclassic-style armchairs. The inner jabots mark the double-hung windows, and the outer jabots lightly touch the floor in classic style. The window treatments flanking the fireplace call attention to the painting hung between them. The red flowers in the swag fabric inspire the bright accents that enliven the formal living room.

Federal-style swags, fabricated from striped silk lined and edged with gray, hang from hooks mounted on either side of the window molding and at ceiling height in the center. The installation visually raises the low ceiling of a 200-year-old house to create airiness enhanced by the open-ground wallpaper. The tails of the swags serve as tailored jabots. In classic style, the tails drop to the midpoint of the window. Wallpaper and chair cushions in complementary patterns pull the room together.

perfect complements

# when elegance counts

For a dressy look, lavishly detailed swags and jabots combine with full drapery side panels to contribute formality that never goes out of fashion. Lined and interlined green-and-white striped silk introduces a desirable ballgown quality. The center and side jabots, trimmed in English dressmaker style, beautifully accentuate the swags and exposed drapery rod and finials. A center rosette and a pair of hand-smocked tiebacks give each window its final embellishment. The result is a grand treatment befitting a dining room of fine antiques, gloriously proportioned windows, and high style.

# bullion-trimmed beauty

In a circa 1760s plantation house, handsomely detailed window treatments imbue the dining room with fresh style while enhancing the architecture and grand proportions of the space. In keeping with the opulence of the furnishings, the lined silk swag wraps the exposed, decoratively fluted gold-tone rod. Side panels neatly frame the windows while bullion fringe lavishly trims the entire swag-and-jabot treatment. Ornate finials and a center tassel hung below the swags add the final stylish touches. Tailored, discreet blinds are used for privacy and sun control.

# tucked and tailored

American colonial style, firmly planted in the late 1700s and early 1800s, continues to have appeal, particularly for collectors of the fine furnishings crafted in the young nation. Moiré swags and extra-long, crisply pleated jabots dress a sitting room anchored by well-known furnishings of the period, including the upholstered Martha Washington-style chair, Baltimore Hepplewhite card table, and Connecticut tall-case clock. The window treatment is a sophisticated, citified version of the shorter, less structured country swags of the period. The swag fabric matches the sunny yellow walls for a pattern-free, polished look.

Wooden drapery rods supported on exposed brackets breathe a touch of American country style into a living room. In keeping with the relaxed yet traditional look, the gracefully draped double swags, fabricated from a lively floral pattern, are detailed with contrasting red fabric ties that add a casual, tied-on look to the design. Tailored side panels are lined with the same red fabric. Mounting the swags on the walls above the windows and using matching fabric for both the swags and the side panels visually heighten the windows. The window-framing treatment also allows the Tudor-style casements to easily open and close. }

# casement solution

Sheer swags gently top the windows of a 19th-century plantation-style bedroom for a feminine interpretation of the tailored Federal style. The sheer fabric contributes to the softly appealing look and easily drapes from the fabric bow (attached below the crown molding) and over the corners of the window frames. The unlined swags impart an ethereal, romantic mood and reflect the room's serene blue and white scheme. With the window treatments as its background, the documentary toile fabric used for the slipper chair, screen, and duvet cover stars in a beautiful fantasy setting.

# swagged and draped

{ Window treatments ensure privacy and style in a sophisticated bedroom. For a simple yet chic presentation, a single length of silk taffeta frames each window and slightly puddles on the carpeted floor. Rosettes, fabricated from contrasting fabric, secure the corners to hidden hardware that is mounted beyond the frames to visually enlarge the casement windows. The rich fabric repeats for the bed hanging, secured by a gold-leafed cornice, and for the gathered bed skirt. When light control is needed, tailored, fabric-covered pull-down shades secure the room.

5

blinds} window style wind

When a room demands simple elegance or architectural sensibility, shutters, shades, and blinds are treatments that deserve serious consideration. All three of these window treatments stand alone beautifully, but each is also flexible enough to be integrated into a more complex or more luxurious statement. In rooms where space around the windows is in short supply, shutters, shades, and blinds can make ideal choices. They stay neatly against the windows, creating a crisp, tailored appearance.

Shutters, perhaps more than any other window treatment, possess the power to enhance the appearance of a home both inside and out. They are classics that work wonders in diverse architectural settings, from colonial- and Cape Cod-style homes to Mediterranean villas and sleek contemporaries. Shutters focus the eye on windows, walls, and moldings. They work well in rooms where windows are gracefully sized, where space is pleasing, and where artisanship, whether simple or complex, shines. Shutters do work magic in many homes, but they are not suited to every home. They may look divine in a 1920s Georgian manor with high ceilings and deep crown moldings, but that doesn't necessarily mean that shutters are right for a 1960s ranch house with low ceilings and oddly proportioned spaces.

Shutters range widely in style, from traditional louvered shutters that perfectly suit historic homes to more contemporary-looking plantation shutters that lend a smart appearance to houses from various architectural periods. Most shutters are custom-made. Even ready-made shutters require a craftsman's hand to precisely tailor them to fit window openings. They can be crafted to accommodate unusually shaped windows, antique or contemporary, including those with demi-lune or Palladian-style tops. Shutters tend to be expensive, but they are a solid investment. Many window treatment styles come and go, but shutters are trend-resistant; they'll maintain their classic good looks for years and years.

Shutters have more than mere beauty to recommend them. Shutters also can be practical choices for rooms where light control is a major concern. In rooms with southern exposure or in any room that receives large doses of light throughout the day, louvered shutters offer the convenience of moderating light and glare precisely and with ease of operation.

Shades are another window treatment well-suited to tailored rooms with good architectural detailing. Simple roller shades provide privacy and light control with no frills (though detail can be artfully added). These shades are most often paired with and hidden beneath attractive valances and/or diaphanous draperies. Newer to the market are attractive natural fiber roller shades in lovely organic weaves and colors.

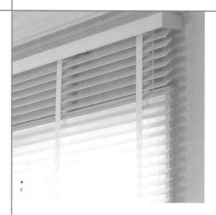

These look smart in casual, relaxed settings and function best in areas where privacy is not a concern and filtered light throughout the day is an asset.

Roman shades also amplify simple elegance and architectural sensibility. The mood they evoke is generally softer and gentler than the mood created by a shutter or blind. The term, Roman shade, once referred specifically to tailored shades with nearly flat folds, but it is now used loosely to encompass both the original style and many hybrids—softly tailored, folding, and draping shades. These appealing shade styles work in diverse decorative settings and can be brilliant in everything from fine silks and damasks to gauzy sheers and coarse burlap. The balloon shade, a close cousin that reached the apex of its popularity not too many years ago, is taking on quieter, less voluminous profiles. The beauty of Roman and balloon shades is often heightened by dressmaker details, contrast lining, piping, and passementerie.

Some Roman shades and balloon shades are not simple to operate and require fluffing after each lifting and lowering; these may not be the best choice for areas where light control and privacy are everyday concerns. In fact, many of these types of shades are made as purely decorative statements. Consider your practical needs before leaping on the Roman shade bandwagon: The beauty of your window treatment may soon cease to thrill you if you have to lift, lower, and straighten several times a day.

Blinds are flexible window treatments that stand alone well, especially in spare modern and casual traditional environments. But blinds also make great partners to drapery panels, and the result of this pairing is often a complex, luxurious, and traditional design statement. Blinds are bountiful: The variety of styles, materials, and colors will satisfy every budget and every decorative style. Simple Venetian blinds and miniblinds are available in a broad range of colors and finishes and have the allure of affordability and rapid delivery. An array of natural fiber blinds is also available. Tried-and-true matchstick blinds are joined by reed, bamboo, hemp, and other textural products that look great on their own or in tandem with drapery panels and/or valances.

Wood blinds, versatile and classic, come in many colors, finishes, and styles. Like matchstick blinds, wood blinds work well in traditional settings and make nice partners to drapery panels. They can fade away with a no-contrast tape, or they can be jauntily plugged into a room's decor with colored or patterned tape. Either way, wood blinds are a smart choice when you want the aesthetics of a shutter without the higher cost. Like shutters, wood blinds lend an architectural air that enhances the interior and exterior of your home. Designers often create a first impression of beauty and serenity by using shutters or wood blinds for all windows that face the street.

# classic roller revisited

In a casual, weekend-home setting, stock pull-down roller shades resolve the problem of sun control—and virtually disappear at the top of the window when views are the number one priority. Unlike popular Roman shades, roller shades have the advantage of rolling discreetly out of the way so that both panes of double-hung windows are clearly visible. White shades match the woodwork and curved bench for minimum contrast. To soften the no-frills treatment, lined, fixed drapery panels attach to the ceiling and frame the bay window. The happy result is a jaunty blue and white scheme perfect for the seaside location.

Inside-mounted, woven bamboo shades diffuse light while imparting a bit of casual tropical style to an eclectically furnished sitting room. The matching header neatly conceals the mounting hardware for a finished look appropriate to the sophisticated furnishings. Such shades can be custom-ordered to fit most windows—helpful in a room such as this one where the windows are different widths. In the spirit of tropical style and the ever-popular British colonial look, a bamboo armchair, a pair of darkly stained tables, stylishly framed art, and animal-motif accessories complete the inviting scene.

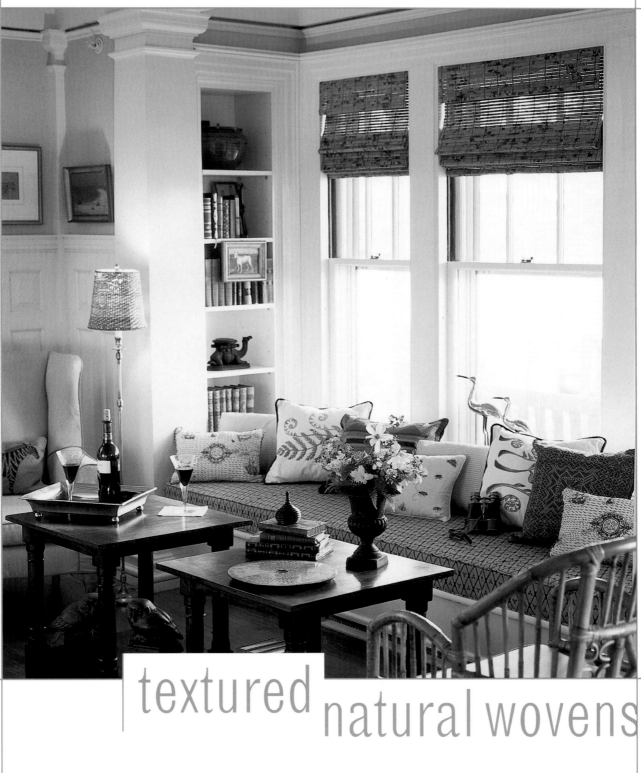

# textured natural wovens

# tailored louvered shutters

Bifold louvered shutters, mounted flush with the window frames and painted to match, work as a tailored backdrop for adjoining living and dining rooms filled with wonderfully disparate elements. In rooms where one-of-a-kind art and artifacts star, the neutral window treatments control the sun with adjustable louvers and create a sense of nighttime privacy, without the distraction of fussy fabrics or fabrications. Classic louvered shutters that blend with the woodwork create a discreet look that pairs with many furniture and art styles, from clearly traditional to coolly contemporary.

# dramatic contemporary

A fabric shade, mounted over a concealed cornice, echoes the sleek style of a sophisticated living room decorated with classic 20th-century furniture and classic poster art. For privacy and sun control, the over-the-window shade lowers for complete coverage. The pale taupe shade contrasts with the white walls and dramatic white sofa for a hint of color. Even in this chic setting, the shade serves a practical purpose by allowing casement windows to open for a breeze. A wagon coffee table and a modern accent table provide interesting shapes and color.

Stylish and always practical, versatile Roman shades fit the bill when a degree of tailored coverage is needed. In this living room, the Roman shade, fabricated from a textured, woven fabric, blends with the subtle wall finish and allows the large painting, dramatic chandelier, and oversize mirror to share design interest. Here, the shade is mounted inside the window frame to take advantage of the nicely detailed trim. Cords and frame-mounted cleats make it easy to adjust these Roman shades, which are typically raised to half the height of the double-hung window during the day.

# working roman shades

# dressy combination

{ Tailored Roman shades work in tandem with draperies for a richer look than shades provide alone. In a serenely neutral living room, Roman shades made from a mossy green damask control daylight and shut out cold winter nights—imparting a touch of pleasing texture as they take care of these chores. Dressier fixed draperies, hung at matching ceiling height, enrich the scene with soft folds and the pretty, classic dressmaker detailing of goblet-header pleating. For a neat daytime look, the Roman shades pleat nicely while the drapery panels slightly puddle on the polished floor—the best of both treatment styles.

A detailed variation of tailored Roman shades, featuring horizontal pleats, translates into a stylish solution for handsome arch-topped windows. Shades are mounted inside the trim at the top of the double-hung windows, taking advantage of the windows' architectural interest. For design detailing and touches of color, the shades are edged in a contrasting trim. Because privacy and sun control are concerns, an opaque fabric allows soft diffusion of light when the shades are down. The combination of tailored design and neutral fabric enhances the contemporary direction of the dining room.

# coverage where it counts

# relaxing the balloon shade

Softly gathered balloon shades dress down a breakfast room with an appealing American country feel. Because the treatment isn't as tightly gathered as Austrian shades, balloon shades lend themselves to such informal settings. Here the balloon shade is mounted at the top of the tall windows, with the handsome molding as the cornice. Oversize tassels add extra accents and call attention to the scallops. The fabric introduces pattern into the room and sets the scheme for the pale green walls, art, and accessories. The ladderback chairs and the gateleg dining table make appropriate furnishings in this inviting room.

# tied with a tassel

{ Interesting printed fabrics with simple fabrications transform rooms, such as hardworking kitchens, into spaces full of personality and welcome. For a kitchen with tile walls, a blue and white cotton print pours on the charm as simple, tied shades and a skirt for the work counter. The lighthearted effect recalls European country kitchens. Fabric shades are mounted inside the window frames, and the lower fabric casing conceals a dowel bar. Cording and tassels provide a neat finish. The softly pleated skirt conceals storage while adding color and an old-fashioned flair to the kitchen.

# tailored pull-up

{ Simply tailored Roman shades, fabricated from loosely woven fabric, soften the stark lines of tall, double-hung windows in a kitchen with intriguing Gothic overtones. The operable shades are mounted inside the window trim to take advantage of the architectural detailing. Because the range hood, with brackets, and diamond-tile backsplash are the focal points, the shades are neutral accents that blend with the walls. Gothic-style chairs, drawn up to the black-granite island, complete the stylish ensemble in a kitchen planned for casual dining and entertaining.

A novelty print fabric, depicting classical Greco-Roman motifs, covers the padded cornice above lavishly gathered, operable balloon shades fabricated into triple scallops. Fabric ruching trims the shades for extra detailing. Extending beyond the side of the window frame, the cornice is mounted below the crown molding to visually raise the window height while providing a neat, finished topper for the balloon shades. The dressy combination is appropriate for a high-style kitchen illuminated by a grand iron and crystal chandelier. Paneling, wallpapered wainscoting, and traditional architectural detailing complete the room.

}

# balloon plus cornice

Offering light control and privacy, understated wood blinds replicate the architectural look of shutters. Wood blinds mounted inside a window frame create a low-key look that works well for a bedroom where a dramatic tester bed takes center stage. The 1-inch-wide slats fold neatly under the header and allow the double-hung window to easily open and close. In a room where the bed makes the design statement, the simple treatment balances the look with a touch of a natural wood tone at the window. The top window is covered with the blinds to soften the effect and to decrease glare.

# simply wood

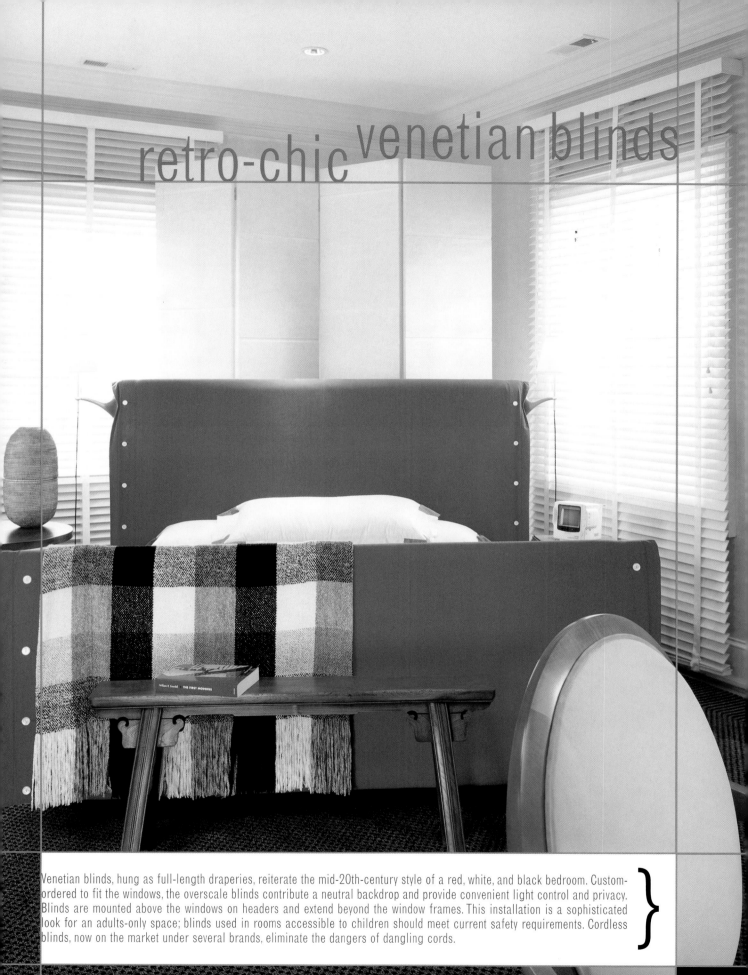

# retro-chic venetian blinds

Venetian blinds, hung as full-length draperies, reiterate the mid-20th-century style of a red, white, and black bedroom. Custom-ordered to fit the windows, the overscale blinds contribute a neutral backdrop and provide convenient light control and privacy. Blinds are mounted above the windows on headers and extend beyond the window frames. This installation is a sophisticated look for an adults-only space; blinds used in rooms accessible to children should meet current safety requirements. Cordless blinds, now on the market under several brands, eliminate the dangers of dangling cords.

# pretty and pleated

Sometimes termed London shades, balloon shades with tails offer a dressy look and detailed fabrication. In a bedroom furnished with fine antiques and inviting upholstered chairs, the shades impart an appropriate refined accent and ensure privacy. Extra detailing includes the goblet-pleated headers, often used in English-style fabrications, and the hand-sewn trim. The blue and white floral fabric, in a dramatic scale, repeats for the tufted Edwardian-style armchair. The overscale blue and white check fabric and the four-poster bed with elaborate finials enhance the crisp, sophisticated scheme.

# shuttered privacy

{ Practical as well as handsome, shutters often are used in rooms such as baths where maintenance and durability are considerations. Operable, louvred shutters, considered a permanent window solution, also offer the benefit of light and privacy control. In an airy master bath, painted shutters match the fresh white trim for a pleasing, unified effect. Decorative window molding contributes to the finished look in the traditional setting. In rooms with odd-sized windows, shutters may need to be custom-ordered to fit window sizes but unify the look.

Fixed balloon shades introduce color and pattern into settings where softness and pattern are the requirements. In a bath where the location ensures privacy, the shades are mounted over the window trim to allow the leaded casement windows to easily open and close. Here the style contributes a floral fabric without dominating the serene scheme. This relaxed treatment, without a header or tight shirring, works well for the cottage ambience—and the cotton fabric holds up well in humid bath conditions. Operable balloon shades or the addition of concealed blinds or pleated shades are options for more privacy.

# softly scalloped

# 6

ndow style {sophisticated

combinations}window sty

There are many beautiful ways to combine window treatments. Some combinations are as simple and affordable as a miniblind topped by an attractive mail-order valance; other combinations, such as the ones featured in this chapter, are more complex, luxurious, and expensive—sometimes fiercely so. In a well-decorated home, continuity and individuality are desirable in furnishings, colors, and window treatments. A house with only one type of chair, one hue, or one style of window treatment would be monotonous. Some window treatments are designed to blend in and others to fade away. A select few are designed to take your breath away. Sophisticated combinations can do all these things, but more often than not, the window treatments that people remember are the ones designed as dramatic focal points in sumptuous settings.

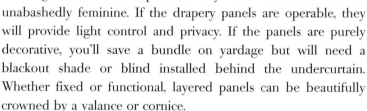

Layered panels, a sheer or loosely woven undercurtain paired with weightier drapery panels, are one classic combination that conveys grace and softness. This treatment is well-suited to rooms where you would like to diffuse natural light, or mask an unattractive view. Although this pairing works throughout the house, layered panels usually conjure images of a romantic master bedroom, a gracious Victorian parlor, or any room where the accent is

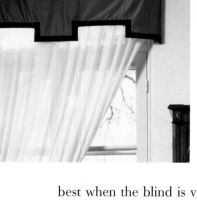

unabashedly feminine. If the drapery panels are operable, they will provide light control and privacy. If the panels are purely decorative, you'll save a bundle on yardage but will need a blackout shade or blind installed behind the undercurtain. Whether fixed or functional, layered panels can be beautifully crowned by a valance or cornice.

Matchstick, bamboo, and other natural-fiber blinds make chic partners to drapery panels, valances, cornices, and swags, especially when you are cultivating a bohemian, organic, or exotic air. The effect is warm, welcoming, and surprisingly rich. Because this pairing looks its best when the blind is visible rather than pulled high and away, it is well suited for libraries, dens, dining rooms, and other spaces where moderate natural light is pleasing and where streaming sunshine is not the goal. Woven shades are another alternative when a degree of light diffusion is the goal. Pretty cabbage rose chintz, crisp document toile, bold tropical-patterned cotton, slubbed Indian silk in saffron yellow, or loosely woven textured linen in a serene neutral hue—whatever the fabric, the effect will be stunning. Topped by a valance, a cornice, or a swag in matching fabric, this treatment is particularly suitable for more formal rooms.

Wood blinds and shutters deliver a classic architectural sensibility when used on their own. Both are excellent choices for a pleasing, tailored treatment that will enhance your windows, especially when viewed from the street. Inside the house, the effect of so many hard treatments may be less pleasing. Adorning a wood blind or shutters with a fabric treatment takes the edge off, and it's a practical pairing too, whether you need easy and precise light modulation or would rather let the sun shine in. This versatile combination conveys almost any decorative style. It works well for relaxed family rooms and children's rooms, breezy master bedrooms and formal living rooms, contemporary kitchens, and old-fashioned baths. The mood depends on the fabric chosen and on the style of the fabric treatment—panels, a valance, a cornice, or swags. It's all up to you. (When blinds or shades are used in a young child's room, remember to follow safety standards; cordless shades are generally best to avoid the hazards of dangling strings.)

Roman shades, balloon shades, and even some roller blinds work perfectly well by themselves. But when you want a more lavish or complex effect, each can be combined in many different and beautiful ways. Drapery panels are classic partners to Roman shades and roller blinds. Depending on the situation, the panels may be functional or merely decorative. (The volume of a balloon shade makes it an unlikely candidate for pairing with draperies. Most of the time, the effect would be overwhelming—too much of a good thing.) A hard cornice, whether metal, wood, or upholstered, works nicely with Roman or balloon shades or with roller blinds. Shapely or fanciful painted cornices produce a charming contrast when paired with the simple structure of a true Roman shade or roller blind. Architectural wood cornices provide a crisp counterpoint, especially to the billowy softness of a balloon shade. Valances and swags, though softer, work much to the same effect. Swags are especially useful when your goal is to unify and soften a group of windows treated with shades or blinds. Depending on the fabric and the swag's design, the look may be grand and opulent or subtle and ephemeral in your chosen setting.

Combination treatments also can spotlight precious or antique fabrics. When yards and yards of a lavish fabric cost too much or are unavailable, a valance or a swag is ideal for showcasing your treasure. In such a case, choose a less costly or more readily available fabric in a complementary weave, weight, color, and pattern to play a supporting role as the side panels.

Patterns used in profusion set the scheme for this pretty, traditional-style living room. With green as the unifying theme, stripes, florals, and document prints mix in fearless abandon. Windows are dressed in a traditional floral silk taffeta that has a vibrant watercolor effect, softening the look of the wood and hardware around the windows and French doors. Silk taffeta plaid lines the drapery panels as well as the swag and jabot. The pinch-pleat panels are attached with rings to the fluted drapery rods. Tasseled trims and rosettes add the extra detailing that defines the beautifully appointed space.

perfectly pretty

# romantic beauties

Decorative French-style hardware makes a forceful design statement in a living room with a decidedly Parisian flavor. With gold-tone circles centering the design, balloon shades with a concealed header are mounted above the French windows. Tassels add artful trim. Side panels with subtle scallops attach with oversize rings to the rod, which is mounted on the molding at ceiling height. Stylized finials playfully punctuate the rods. With the striped, watery silk as the fabric starting point, a discreet mix of solids, florals, and stripes completes a room of Old-World charm and ambience.

# matched to perfection

Alluding to castles and the Gothic Revival style, striped silk cornices with a crenellated shape edged in dark piping bring unexpected boldness to sheer drapery panels. The rich treatment reflects the traditional style of a room that includes fine antiques, such as the mahogany secretary, while also adding playful punch. Cornices are mounted above the windows on concealed headers. The unlined sheers are gently pulled aside to expose the tall French doors. The effect is one of chic yet simple sophistication, appropriate for a drawing room furnished with art, antique books, and fine collected treasures.

# cornice-topped sheers

# natural pairing

For a room of exotic treasures with Asian influences, fixed, self-pleated drapery panels attach to bamboo rods mounted below the crown molding. The treatment visually raises the windows and helps balance the proportions of a large room with an 8-foot ceiling. The panels frame the windows and soften the hard edges of the wood and metal furnishings. Operable woven shades are mounted below the rod for a degree of privacy and light control. The inspired mix introduces additional textures into a room where the combination of fabrics and rugs is the focal point of a monochromatic scheme.

{ To dress a large bay window in a traditional library, a fully gathered valance with a fabric-trimmed header tops fixed, matching floral drapery panels trimmed in braid. The panels' lining of green, red, and yellow plaid taffeta is sewn to wrap around to the front of the curtains, providing a beautiful frame for the deep bay. For another custom touch, muslin bows and wood tassels, imported from England, detail the unlined scalloped Roman shades. Although the window treatment fabric does not repeat, its rich colors set the scheme for the novelty print used on the club chairs and the exotic paisley print that covers the sofa.

# highlighting a bay

# softly accented

Pale colors refresh the traditional style while pinch-pleat drapery panels and balloon shades refine the mood of quiet sophistication. Panels attach with rings to the tailored drapery rods, which are detailed with ball finials. Simple balloon shades are mounted above the tall, double-hung windows for a finished effect that conceals the tops of the windows. The low-key approach allows decorative pillows and accent fabrics, such as the overscale check used on the exposed-wood armchair, to stand out in the subtle scheme.

# tropical punch

While slatted woven bamboo shades do the real work of controlling light and privacy, tropical-print drapery panels have the fun: introducing pattern and definition to a living room with overtones of classic British colonial style. Real bamboo poles, serving as drapery hardware, are mounted on the window frame. Drapery panels, sized to touch the sill, are tied on for an appealing casual look. Custom-ordered bamboo shades with self-headers fit snugly inside the window frames. The bamboo motifs of the shades repeat for the desk and magazine rack and for the faux-bamboo lamp bases.

In a powder room of surprisingly modest proportions, vertically striped pink panels lined in cabbage rose chintz draw the eye up to the crown molding. Panels graze the floor, visually heightening the space. The extra flourish of a jabot on the lushly swagged valance, along with the ruffled and rosette trims in a complementary green and pink cotton check, recalls the grandeur of 18th-century French interiors. Painted in mottled shades of pink to match the drapery fabric, the crown molding blends with the luxe window treatment below. The faux beadwork on the walls continues the drama.

# french finery

easy elegance

A draped swag and jabot layered over silk curtain panels dress a tall window and balance the wall's dramatic paint treatment. For definition, the contrast-lined and piped crossed swag is hung above the window with the matching jabot trailing down to baseboard height. Trimmed silk curtains also cross and puddle. Rosettes, detailed with ruched trim, serve as tiebacks. The golden and taupe tones of the fabric repeat for the mottled wall finish and the painted panel detailing. French-style furniture completes a chic scene that evokes the romance of a European city apartment.

# color-block statement

{ For an East-meets-West dining room that celebrates the best of fusion design, drapery panels are fabricated from mocha, fawn, and pale blue Indian silk. In keeping with the simplicity of the room's design, panels are gathered without headers on concealed drapery hardware mounted inside the frames of the French windows. The subtle combination of the silk draperies enhances the ambience of the sophisticated, cleanly designed space. Walls also feature the three soft colors: A mocha chair rail gives way to fawn above, and a striking 2-foot-tall palmetto-leaf design is stenciled in cream over the pale blue border.

A combination of a pull-down shade and well-tailored pinch-pleat drapery panels reinforces the clean lines of a sunny breakfast nook anchored by banquette seating. With a cornice header for neatness, the shade is covered in a jaunty check and features gentle curves and edging trim. Flanking, fixed drapery panels are detailed with bands of the checkered fabric and trim to unify the look and to relax the straight-line geometry of the table and ottomans. Side panels of the nook are ribboned message boards covered in a neutral fabric that repeats the soft tones of the window treatment.

# clean contemporary

# high-flying valances

For a new take on the simple pairing of unstructured valances and drapery side panels, contrast-edged valances hang from ceiling-mounted hooks to visually elevate an 8-foot ceiling. To avoid interfering with a covered radiator, only the valance dresses the windows at the end of the small room, creating a serendipitous variation of the full window treatment. Operable drapery panels dress up the windows on the remaining two sides of the sunny space. The printed, damask-style fabric in sunny yellow and white brightens the country-style furnishings. A stylized animal-print slipcover introduces a lighthearted touch to the setting.

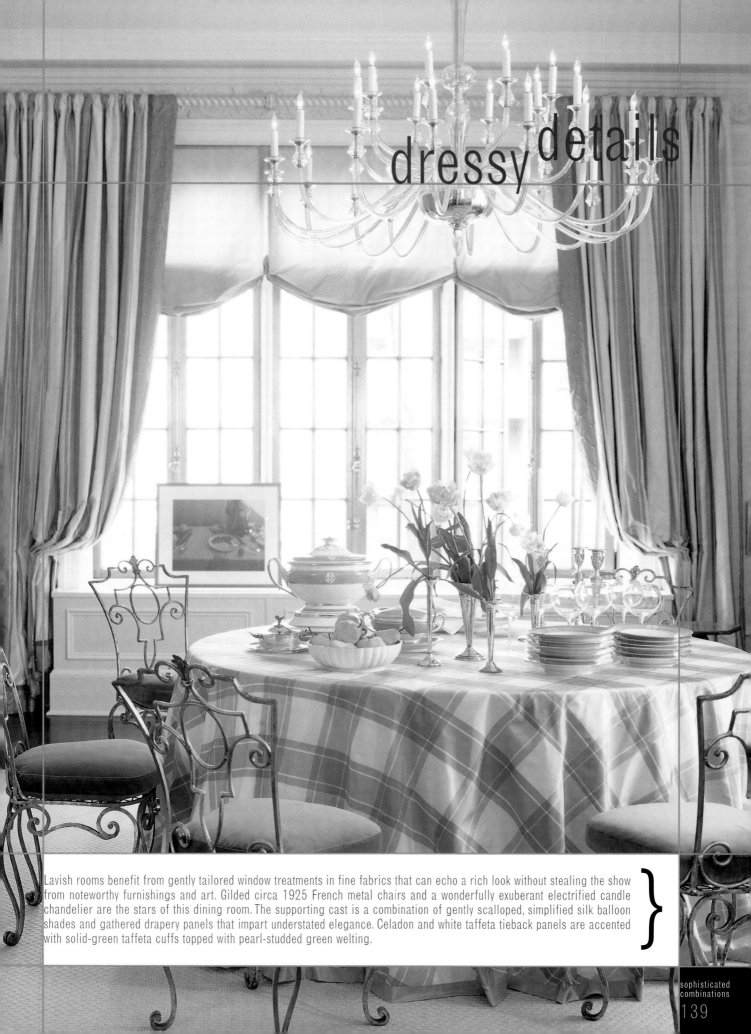

# dressy details

Lavish rooms benefit from gently tailored window treatments in fine fabrics that can echo a rich look without stealing the show from noteworthy furnishings and art. Gilded circa 1925 French metal chairs and a wonderfully exuberant electrified candle chandelier are the stars of this dining room. The supporting cast is a combination of gently scalloped, simplified silk balloon shades and gathered drapery panels that impart understated elegance. Celadon and white taffeta tieback panels are accented with solid-green taffeta cuffs topped with pearl-studded green welting.

# inspired collaboration

{ In a bedroom of luminous tints and unabashed elegance, a shirred cornice header tops a gently scalloped swag, precisely tailored jabots, and operable drapery panels. The cornice is trimmed in a tailored braid, and tasseled passementerie details the swags and jabots. A centered rosette accents the design. Although elaborate, the window treatment appears appropriately restrained as the silk fabric and trim blend with the tastefully sponged and stenciled wall treatment. The effect is one of luxury, but not glitz, for a quietly tasteful room of French-style furnishings.

# romantic revival

A stunning silk stripe unifies a guest room, appearing in the high-style window treatment and in the lining for the tie-on bed hangings. To dress the stately French windows, the silk stripe is fabricated into gathered balloon shades; it also hangs as side panels. The shapely finial and decorative rings contribute detailing to the effect. The silk fabric works equally well as the lining for the panels that define iron twin beds. Along with the Aubusson rug and oil portraits, the classic fabrications ground the room in a feeling of continental luxury.

A triple swag, detailed with matching fabric rosettes, and softly tailored drapery panels dress a bedroom retreat where style and relaxation are the goals. Because furnishings are low-key yet elegant, the elaborate combination of drapery fabrication contributes design interest and calls attention to the drama of the tall window. For visual continuity, the pale fabric blends with the wall color. Small-scale furnishings, an overscale mirror, and well-edited artwork finish a room that offers privacy, calm, and quiet good taste. Blackout shades, concealed under the swag, can be used for nighttime privacy.

}

## swagged and draped

Fully gathered valances and matching, operable drapery panels reinforce the mood of quiet, serene luxury in a master bedroom. The fabric—and the fabrications—set a decorating direction that's relaxed yet sophisticated. To add a look of height to the room, the softly gathered valances are hung at the ceiling line. Piping at the hem provides a nicely tailored finish. Echoing the window treatment, the bed hanging also is suspended from a fabric-covered cornice that is mounted at the ceiling. The upholstered headboard and banded table skirt add design interest to the pale, monochromatic palette.

# privacy please

Tailored balloon shades guarantee privacy for a master bath dominated by a striking bay with casement windows. To blend with the pale yellow walls in a luminous eggshell finish, the drapery panels are raw silk, and the shades are a blending shade of brushed cotton. The effect is subtler than an all-silk treatment but equally chic. For a neat finish, the operable shades and the drapery panels are attached with rings to the drapery rods. The drapery provides a sophisticated backdrop for the room's other decorating attributes, including the beaded flower-motif light fixture and the stenciled limestone-tile floor.

A botanical-motif, fern print fabric inspires the scheme for a bedroom decorated in the tropical spirit. Because of the open background and the simplicity of the ferns, the detailed fabric works equally well for the smooth cornice and the operable, floor-length drapery side panels. The cornice serves the practical purposes of concealing the drapery hardware and visually balancing the vaulted ceiling. Pairs of louvered shutters, painted white, control light and views while reinforcing the tropical mood. The fabric repeats for the armchairs and ottoman to unify the scheme.

## stylish simplicity

indow style {working with

professionals} window st

For too many people, window treatments come as an afterthought, something considered only when the room has been painted, furnished, and fluffed. Yet window treatments are essential to a room's beauty, comfort, and finish. For the most pleasing look, treatments must be appropriate to the architectural style and the interior design style of your home. Planning them as part of your overall design results in a room that is unified, a room that is both practical and polished.

If your budget permits, seek the help of an interior designer. This is not industry propaganda, but rather some of the best decorating advice you'll ever get. Planning and installing can be difficult, especially if you want drapery or shade styles that incorporate complex pleating, lined valances, and dressmaker details. The window treatments that make you smile or sigh as you leaf through design magazines or books are delectable, but most of these are, in fact, the product of painstaking professional planning and execution.

Hiring an interior designer to help you make window treatment decisions is not so much a luxury as a smart investment in the lasting beauty and comfort of your home. Window treatment design is complicated. Design professionals understand fabrics, trim, dressmaker details, and other intricacies. They've done it all before, so they have a solid understanding of what works where, and when, and why. Almost magically, a savvy designer can make small windows look bigger, make awkward windows appear more proportional to the rooms in which they are located, or put an unfortunate view of a neighbor's air-conditioning unit gently out of sight and mind.

Designers understand light control, privacy, and insulation—issues that may seem mundane, but ones that can make all the difference in your day-to-day life. Designers know the importance of lining and interlining, when each is vital to the overall effect and when they are frivolous, unnecessary expenses. Designers also understand when less is more—when an architectural wood cornice above a beautiful mullioned window is all that's needed for a splendid effect or when a truly breathtaking view can stand and deliver entirely on its own. These same decorating experts know when, in the immortal words of interior designer Charles Faudree of Tulsa, "too much is not enough." There are situations where matchstick blinds paired with pretty chintz panels, and crowned by a cascading valance with contrast lining and crystal beaded trim make a room sparkle brilliantly; in other places the

blinds themselves are all you need. Knowing which is which—that is this expertise you pay for. Design professionals have access to a wonderful world of fabrics that, without them, you do not. Many of the most beautiful fabrics, hardware, and passementerie are available only "to the trade"—which means no designer, no access. More appealing fabrics are available at retail than ever before, but the breadth, depth, and quality of standard retail offerings do not approach what you will find through a designer. As with window treatments themselves, there are interior designers to suit every taste and budget. At one end of the spectrum, you will find designers who specialize in exorbitantly expensive and expansive projects that take years to complete; at the other end are designers who specialize in one room or even one window treatment at a time. There are excellent (and not-so-excellent) designers at every point along this spectrum. Careful research, planning, and organization on your part will pay off as you begin interviewing interior designers. If you have a good sense of what you want and examples to show, you're much more likely to find a great fit—a designer who will be in tune with your taste, timetable, budget, and personality.

Ask for designer recommendations from friends and colleagues whose homes and window treatments you admire. Designer showhouses, home furnishings boutiques, and your local chapter of ASID (American Society of Interior Designers) are other sources for information about local design professionals. Reputable interior designers will discuss their fees and how they operate up front. They welcome questions, clearly explain how the design process works, detail what their expectations are, and describe the parameters of the services they perform. Professional designers charge for their services in various ways, including hourly rates, flat project fees, percentages of the total project cost, and hourly fees combined with a small markup on the goods you purchase through them.

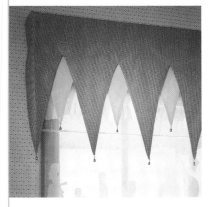

Experienced designers will come to interviews armed with a portfolio of their work. This gives you an opportunity to examine real examples of work they have done and ask them to explain what they did and why. Always ask for references and contact a few. This will give you a good idea of what it's like working with a particular designer. Show—don't just tell—a designer what you want. Clippings from magazines or tabbed pages in books go a long way in communicating your ideas of what a swag with jabots or a balloon shade with fringe means to you.

If an interior designer is not in your plans, consider the services of a well-regarded drapery workroom or a professional seamstress. Unless your window treatment designs are simple and you are accomplished at measuring, cutting, sewing, and finishing and own a quality sewing machine, a workroom or experienced seamstress is far better equipped to make your windows look their best. Find a good workroom the same way you research designers: Ask those you trust for recommendations; then discuss fees and inspect samples of actual work done by each workroom. Many drapery workrooms are run by creative professionals who have access to the same fabrics, hardware, and trim that designers use. If you find such a drapery workroom, take advantage of its design expertise and explore the full range of its design services. If you are working with a seamstress, consider whether she has sufficient experience to do your window treatments justice. Many seamstresses are capable of making simple drapery panels or valances, but when you begin adding inverted pleats, contrast lining, leading-edge border treatments, and other complicated techniques, a drapery workroom is probably a safer bet. The finished window treatment should be utterly professional. Don't risk an amateurish result. A bad window treatment is worse than no window treatment at all.

How do you choose the window treatment that is most appropriate for your room? Begin by pondering the following points:

•What is the architectural style of your home? Like it or not, the architecture of your home should play a part in the window treatment you choose.

•What features do you want to play up—or down? Take stock of the room: its size, its ceiling height, any special moldings, the fireplace, the window placement and style, the floors, the size and placement of doorways, and anything else that gives the room its basic character. Window treatments can call attention to a room's inherent assets, such as beautifully milled crown moldings or a lofty ceiling. Conversely, window treatments also can make up for a room's deficits by rescaling an awkwardly sized window, masking its flaws, or drawing the eye away from features you'd prefer to minimize.

•What colors are/will be at play in the room?

•What patterns and fabrics are already there?

•What is the general style of furnishings?

•What other rooms are visible from this space? What colors/moods/window treatments are in these other rooms? Adjacent rooms should harmonize with, not mimic, one another.

Your answers to the preceding questions will provide a basic style framework. Also consider the following practicalities:

**How is the room used, and how often is it used?** How you use the room is critical in determining the most practical window treatment for your needs. A guest room, for instance, is a smart place to showcase beautiful but difficult-to-operate window treatments that might be frustratingly inconvenient if installed in a high-use area such as the family room. Unless you have a large amount of time and patience, avoid treatments that require fluffing every time they are adjusted. Some higher-maintenance treatments include balloon shades, relaxed Roman shades, panels that puddle luxuriously at the floor, and draperies with valances that attach to the rod or rings. These styles are best suited to areas where the window treatments are primarily decorative and infrequently operated, such as formal living or dining rooms.

**Does the room have special light considerations?** If a room receives sunlight throughout the day, easy and precise modulation of the window treatment is fundamental. In such situations, operable shutters and blinds make ideal choices. They allow you to admit exactly the right amount of light, cut glare, and avoid the problem of fading fabrics.

If you have a room that doesn't receive much natural light, preserving and amplifying what little light the window lets in is key. Even in a dressy situation, an elegant cornice or a diaphanous swag draped across a distinctive rod with finials may be all you want or need.

**Does the room have special privacy or insulation requirements?** Master bedrooms and media rooms often require drapery treatments with special lining and interlining for practicality, comfort, and opulence. Where blackout blinds or shades are used, you'll want a top treatment, such as a valance, to conceal the hardware.

**Is the window an odd size?** If your window is awkwardly shaped, certain drapery and shade styles create the artful illusion of added height, width, or proportion. Mounting draperies with a valance well above where the window actually ends gives a shorter window new stature. The same can be done without a valance for windows in need of less stretch. A narrow window can be visually widened by solid drapery panels (rather than sheers), made wider than the window and never fully drawn to reveal where the window ends and the walls begin.

**What is your budget?** Shutters are expensive. So are draperies that use yards and

yards of special fabric. Blinds and window treatments that use fabric more sparingly are more affordable. However, if a top treatment isn't required to conceal blinds or shades, stylish drapery panels call for less fabric and less fabrication than styles with elaborate swags, pleats, rosettes, and jabots. Sometimes the most chic solutions are simple drapery panels that maximize the beauty of a fabulous fabric, such as silk.

## Will children be using the room?

Certain blinds, Roman shades, and other treatments have operational cords that can be dangerous to young children. Steer clear of these treatments in rooms where children will be. If you want to use blinds, check that they meet current safety requirements, or purchase the newer, cordless models available through major manufacturers and at retailers including mass merchants and home center stores.

If the treatment is for children's rooms and the children are old enough to operate a window treatment themselves, select a style that they'll be able to manipulate easily on their own, such as cotton drapery panels on simple open-and-close rings.

## Do you have pets? Would your dog

nest in the opulent silk draperies puddling on the floor in your dining room? Will the cats see the textural woven shades in your home office as attractive new scratching posts? Don't invite trouble. If you have young or overactive pets, consider simple blinds or shades instead of floor-length fabric window treatments.

## Is your view absolutely stunning?

Sometimes a window, its orientation, and its view are all so compelling that the window is best left undressed. It's rare, but it does happen.

When you've answered all the questions above, you'll have a general idea of what window treatments are most appropriate for your room and the way you live.

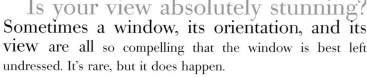

## WHAT PROS KNOW ABOUT FABRIC:

Silk—When you want shimmer, shine, and ballgown elegance, there is no fabric that compares to silk. Silk taffeta panels are synonymous with rich, traditional rooms, and they're a perfect choice when the mood is formal. Silk needn't be pigeonholed as a dress-only fabric, however. It can be used to fresh effect, even in fairly relaxed and contemporary settings. Certain silks, such as slubbed Indian silks, are not terribly expensive, and their textural weave suits casual styles. In general, silk is expensive, but it is also easy to work with. There is one serious drawback: Silk is easily damaged by moisture or sunlight. To foster long life, it should be lined and interlined. However, if sun exposure is not a major concern or if you like a more casual approach, consider using decorative Indian sari cloth, which is often draped or hung unlined.

Cotton—Depending on its weave, pattern, color, and finish, this versatile fabric can present a quite formal appearance (glazed cottons), a very casual look (cotton duck), and everything in between. Cotton makes lovely draperies, curtains, valances, and shades. Inexpensive cotton is easily dressed up when paired with striking hardware, chic border fabrics, and lush trim. Cotton velvets are weighty and luxurious. Cotton chintz requires special care because exposure to water and steam can remove its characteristic sheen. When used in a dressy environment, cotton drapery panels should be interlined to maintain their shape and to hang properly.

Linen—This is another versatile fabric that can be used in relaxed or more formal settings. Linen often delivers rich texture and sophistication to a room. Like cotton, it can be used for simple treatments, including drapery panels, swags, valances, and shades, or it can be elevated with fancy hardware, opulent border fabrics, and trimmings. For formal draperies, linen panels are usually best interlined. Linen is a more vulnerable fabric than cotton: Moisture can cause stretching, heat can cause shrinkage, and wrinkling can be a concern. Still, designers do love linen, and its great look makes it worth the risks. Linen-and-cotton blends are also widely marketed for draperies.

Wool—Wool is an appealing fabric that can be as rich and substantial as a thick flannel or as light and breezy as wool challis sheers. Wool is less commonly used for window treatments than many other fabrics are, but it has definite merits. It hangs well and folds gracefully, and its weightiness lends warmth and welcome to any setting, from traditional to contemporary. Wool draperies should be protected from heat vents and moisture.

Synthetics—More unusual and attractive synthetic fabrics and synthetic blends are on the market than ever before. They generally cost less, fade less, and are easier to clean than natural fabrics. Shrinkage, if any, tends to be more even. However, synthetic fabrics usually don't drape as well as natural fabrics. In addition, drapery workrooms report that synthetics, including many synthetic sheers, can be nightmarish to sew. Use caution when selecting a synthetic fabric. If you have any inkling that a synthetic fabric may not drape, fold, or pleat properly or that the fabric may not be long-lived, discuss your concerns with your designer or drapery workroom.

Cotton/Poly or Viscose Blends—These fabrics can be "the best of all worlds," according to interior designer Fiona Newell Weeks. A heavily woven blend doesn't need interlining and can make a

great drapery, given the right header or panel style. But don't expect such a fabric to drape. Heavy blend fabrics make good flat panels or Roman shades. If the blend fabric is thin and light, it will not make a good Roman shade; instead try a softly draping balloon shade. If the fabric comes first, Fiona Newell Weeks adds, choose the treatment style accordingly, and vice versa.

Burlap—Magazines are full of delightful draperies, shades, and valances fabricated from inexpensive burlap and, sometimes, hemp. These window treatments can be wonderfully textural, fun, and exceedingly affordable, but they are not long-lived. Even with lining, which makes the treatment much more expensive, burlap has a distinctive odor, it discolors, and it deteriorates rapidly, especially in sunny locations. Burlap is also extremely fibrous, making it difficult to sew (one designer suggests wearing goggles when fabricating). However, burlap does have a pleasing natural look. It is not a long-term solution, but it can be perfect for temporary treatments.

## WHAT THE PROS KNOW ABOUT CONSTRUCTION AND LINING:

Great artisanship: This is critical to the impact of the finished product. Even if you select the finest fabric and trim along with the most elegant hardware, a drapery will still be a dismal failure if it isn't well-made. Go with the very best workroom or experienced seamstress

you can afford. Better yet, leave finding this resource to a trained professional. Interior designers stress that lining and interlining are almost always worth the added expense. Almost every drapery, including most very casual treatments, will benefit from lining. Lining hides seams, helps draperies hang gracefully, and lends a finished look. Interlining bolsters most draperies, although some breezy, casual styles, such as the popular sheers, are candidates for this extra layer. "Lining and interlining can make even an inexpensive fabric look like a million bucks," says one East Coast designer. Lining and interlining both lend a palpable touch of quality. They are also a good investment: A window treatment that is lined or interlined looks good longer.

To trim or not to trim: When a fabric is captivating and the drapery design is utterly elegant, billowy and puddling at the floor, who needs trim? Certainly there are situations where a fabric stands alone so beautifully that trim would be mere clutter. But these situations are rare. Most soft window treatments, especially draperies, valances, and shades, benefit from some form of trim, whether it is self-piping, a contrast fabric border, or rich passementerie— gimp, cording, beading, or tassels. The key is to select trim that suits the drapery fabric and style as well as the scale of the treatment and window. If the room is quiet, dressing a window treatment with opulent trim may inject vital spark and polish. If

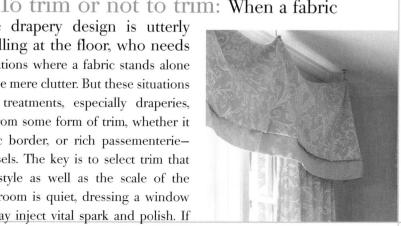

the room is brimming with furniture, color, pattern, and accessories, a simple trim may be the most tasteful choice.

**Dressmaker details:** Like trim, dressmaker details lend beauty and charm—and expense. Treatments fabricated with simple folds cost less than those with pleating (pinch pleats, inverted pleats, box pleats, and knife-pleats are popular details). Unusual draping techniques, shirred headers, and other complicated fabrications raise the price of dressing a window. Dressmaker details shine brightly in rich traditional rooms, but well-chosen ones are also chic in clean-lined transitional spaces.

**Proper measurements:** If you can, leave measurements to professionals. If you take measurements yourself, use a steel measuring tape. For inside-mounted treatments, measure the width of the opening at the top, middle, and bottom. Record the narrowest measurement. Follow a similar procedure for measuring length, checking at the left, middle, and right of the window opening. For outside mounts, measure the width of the opening and add at least 3 inches to each side measurement. Measure the length of the opening and add at least 2 inches in height for hardware and overlap. Double-check for accuracy. To measure drop for draperies or curtains, measure from where you intend to install the rod to where you want draperies or curtains to fall. For width, measure the length of the rod. To calculate the length of a swag, measure

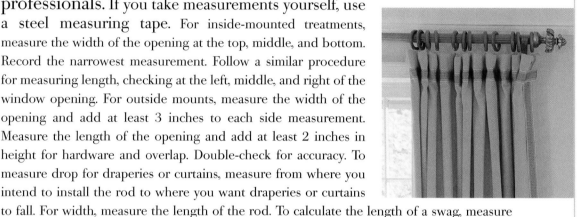

the distance from the bottom of the drapery ring, rod, or other mount to the desired length of the swag. Multiply that measurement by 2 and add 10 inches to each side if you want the fabric to puddle at the floor. Measure the width of the area to be covered; add that figure to the length for the total yardage.

**Care to ensure long wear:** Don't dry-clean draperies and fabric shades that are lined or interlined. Interlining can shrink, swell, and pucker, so the treatments may not hang properly after the cleaning. Designers recommend gently vacuuming panels and spot cleaning if necessary. Shutters and wood blinds can be dusted or wiped with a mild soapy solution.

**Restyling window treatments:** To breathe new life into your rooms, window treatments are a great place to start. However well-made or timeless your draperies may be, one day you will find that they need refreshing or replacing. If your draperies are too short, you can add a complementary or contrasting band of fabric along the bottoms; then use the same new fabric for a new valance, cornice, or swag. If you like the fabric but consider the drapery style tired, install a new rod and/or rings, add trim, or mount appealing tiebacks. If you are tired of a drapery's header style, you can hide it with a soft valance or a hard cornice. Or retire the draperies and use their ample yardage for new valances, swags, shades, or cornices.

## Credits

Pages 8-21: Designer: Fiona Newell Weeks, Fiona Newell Weeks Interiors, 7804 Masters Drive, Potomac, MD 20854. 301/983-6989. Photographer: Gordon Beall. Field editor: Colleen Scully.

# window style